TOMFOOLERY
Trickery and Foolery with Words

Collected from American Folklore
by Alvin Schwartz

The New York Times Outstanding Book
for Children 1973

"A rambunctious compilation of traditional tom-foolery, that is corny, contrary and downright infectious."

—*Kirkus Reviews*

"*Tomfoolery* contains riddles old and new, corny jokes, word puzzles, tangletalk, plays on words, delightfully silly poems and an assorted selection of other verbal nonsense that children have enjoyed for generations."

—*Elementary English*

"This collection of humorous word games, tricks and riddles is delightful."

—*Library Journal*

"Wonderfully, zany illustrations by Glen Rounds. It's a total success."

—*The New York Times*

TOMFOOLERY

TOMFOOLERY
TRICKERY AND FOOLERY
WITH WORDS

COLLECTED FROM AMERICAN FOLKLORE
BY ALVIN SCHWARTZ
ILLUSTRATED BY GLEN ROUNDS

A SKYLARK BOOK

RLI: $\dfrac{\text{VLM 3 (VLR 3-5)}}{\text{IL 3+}}$

TOMFOOLERY: TRICKERY AND FOOLERY WITH WORDS

*A Bantam Skylark Book / published by arrangement with
J. B. Lippincott Company*

PRINTING HISTORY

Lippincott edition published April 1973

2nd printing . . . .*May 1973*
3rd printing . . . .*May 1974*
4th printing . . . .*September 1975*

Bantam Skylark edition / October 1976

COPYRIGHT CREDITS

FOR NAN

Contents

Trickery and Foolery

The tricks in this book do not involve hiding some-body's lunch or nailing his or her sneakers to the floor. Instead they depend on words, and, at times, on a pinch or some other friendly gesture.

Some of these tricks with words are questions that will make your friends feel slightly foolish when they give the "right" answers.

Some are riddles with answers that no one in his right mind would give.

And some are tales with such odd twists and turns, with such unexpected endings, they would fool almost anybody.

No one knows who created these tricks or just where they came from. Nor does anyone know just how old most of them are, except that some are very old. What we do know is that they are part of the games, songs, beliefs, and other traditions we call our folklore.

As with all folklore, these tricks have been passed by word of mouth from one person to another. In fact, some are tricks your parents and their parents knew when they were growing up.

Usually people play these tricks when they want to make things more lively. But many know only a few. If that is your problem, this book could help.

Alvin Schwartz

Princeton, New Jersey

TOMFOOLERY

1.

IF FROZEN WATER
IS ICED WATER,
WHAT IS
FROZEN INK?

The answer is, of course, iced ink. Which few people are willing to admit. The folklorists call this a catch or a trap. A good catch will make someone look silly if he isn't on his toes. It also will make him laugh or groan. In this case the catch is a question. But there are many kinds to try.

Take any number.
Add ten.
Subtract three.
Now close your eyes.
(Your friend closes his eyes.)
Dark, isn't it!

Please add these up:
    One ton of sawdust.
    One ton of old newspaper.
    Four tons of string.
    One-half ton of fat.
    Have you got all that in your head?
Yes.
I thought so.

ABRAHAM LINCOLN USED TO TRY THIS ONE:

If three pigeons are sitting on a fence, and you shoot and
    kill one of them, how many will be left?
Two, of course.
No, there won't. For the other two will fly away.

If you were walking in a field
and there weren't any trees to climb
and you didn't have a gun
and you saw a bear heading for you,
what would you do?
Run.

With a bear behind?

I know a fellow who had snew in his blood.
What's snew?
Nothing. What's new with you?

I bet I can jump across the street.
I bet you can't.
(Walk across the street and jump.)

Is your house on _____ Street?
Yes.
Better hurry up and move it! There's a car
    coming!

Ask me if I'm a boat.
Are you a boat?
Yes. Now ask me if I'm an
    airplane.
Are you an airplane?
No, I just told you I'm
    a boat!

As you tell this story, hold one of your palms in front of you and trace your journey with a finger, using the creases as if they were streets. Substitute the names of streets where you live for those used in the account below.

YOU: My mother sent me to the store to buy a bottle of vinegar and a pound of butter. I walked down Main Street, then over to George Street, then down Lincoln Avenue. When I got to the store, I bought the butter and the vinegar, and the man put them in a bag, and I started to walk home.

I walked back down Lincoln Avenue and then over to George Street. When I finally reached Main Street, I tripped on a broken sidewalk and dropped the bag and broke the bottle of vinegar.

Do you know what butter and vinegar smell like when they are mixed together?

YOUR FRIEND: No.

you: Like this!

Ask a friend to play a number game with you. You start by saying, "I one it." Then he says, "I two it." And the counting continues:

I three it.

I four it.

I five it.

I six it.

I seven it.

I eight it.

Oh, you ate that old dead horse!

Do you know something?

No, what?

Awful dumb, aren't you!

Will you remember me in fifty years?
Yes.
Will you remember me in twenty years?
Yes.
Will you remember me in ten years?
Yes.
Will you remember me in five years?
Yes.
Will you remember me next year?
Yes.
Will you remember me next month?
Yes.
Will you remember me next week?
Yes.
Will you remember me tomorrow?
Yes.
Will you remember me in another minute?
Yes.
Will you remember me in another second?
Yes.
Knock, knock.
Who's there?
You forgot me already?

If I lived up here

and you lived down here,

would you come up and see me some time?

Would you hit someone after he surrenders?
No.
(Hit your friend, then announce:) I surrender!

Hey, your shirttail's on fire!
It is?
(Pull your friend's shirt out, then say:)
     Now it's out!

Watch out! There's a henweigh on your neck!
What's a henweigh?
About three pounds.

Would you like to join a secret society?
OK.
Good! It's called the Royal Order of Siam. Just bow five
    times and repeat these Siamese words:

OWAH TAGOO SIAM!

I can make you into an old-fashioned Indian.
How?
(Raise your right hand, keep your head high, then say:)
    How!

Point to the center of the palm of one of your hands. Explain to your friend that the spot you are pointing to is really a baby and that the baby is brand-new and delicate and needs a lot of rest.

Then say:

"Father says, 'Don't touch the baby!'

"Mother says, 'Don't touch the baby!'

"Brother says, 'Don't touch the baby!'

"Sister says, 'Don't touch the baby!' "

And each time point to the spot.

Then ask your friend, "Where is the baby?"

When he points to the spot or touches it, shout, "DON'T TOUCH THE BABY!" and smack his hand.

This old tale is both a catch and a "scare story." Mark Twain called it "a lovely story to tell." For the best results tell it at night in the dark to at least two or three other people. It goes this way:

There was this old man who had a golden arm because he had lost his real arm in an accident. And when he died his wife wanted to get that arm so that she could become rich.

So she decided she would wait until he was buried and then go and sneak into the graveyard one night and dig up the body and get the arm.

And so she did it. But then she started having these bad dreams and she would hear all these strange noises. And then one night, with the wind blowing and howling and everything, she heard this voice way out in the distance.

And it was like, "Whoooo stole my golden arm? Whooooo stole my golden arm?"

And she locked all the doors and the windows in the house and got into bed and pulled the blankets up to her

head and lay there, scared to death.

And the voice kept getting closer and closer, moaning and groaning, "Whoooo stole my golden arm? Whooooo stole my golden arm?"

And then the door downstairs opened and she heard these footsteps and they got louder and louder and louder.

And then the door to her bedroom opened and the footsteps came closer and closer. And she lay there shaking. Then suddenly she heard the voice again, only now it was right next to her whispering in her ear.

"Whoooo stole my golden arm?" it moaned. "Whoooo stole my golden arm? Whooooo? Whoooooo?"

(At this point pause. Then grab the person next to you and shout:)

"YOU DID!"

Do you collect stamps?
Yes.
Here's one for your
        collection.
(Stamp on one of your friend's feet.)

    If your friend says "no," then you say, "Well, here's one to start with," and take the necessary steps.

Three little monkeys sat on a fence. Their names were Doe, Rey, and Me. Doe and Rey fell off. Who was left?

Me.

I want to tell you a story, but to help you must say "Just
    like me" each time I stop.

OK.

I went up one flight of stairs.

Just like me.

I went up two flights of stairs.

Just like me.

I went up three flights of stairs.

Just like me.

I went up four flights of stairs.

Just like me.

I went into a little room.

Just like me.

I looked out a window.

Just like me.

I saw a monkey.

Just like me.

JUST like you!

To play this trick you need somebody who is wearing a tie. If all goes well this is what will happen.

What does a ship do when it enters a harbor?
Ties up.
(Flip up your friend's tie.)

But if your friend says "Toots its horn" or "Docks," or gives some other answer that doesn't help, then you must tell him, "It also does something else—ties up!" and proceed as planned.

I know what you're going to say next.
What?
That's what!

I bet I can make you say "black."
I bet you can't.
What's the color of the American flag?
Red, white, and blue.
See, I told you I could make you say "blue."
No, you said I'd say "black."
You just did.

I bet you can't stick your tongue out
    and touch your nose.
(Your friend tries, but fails.)
I'll show you how. (Stick your tongue out, and
    touch your nose with your finger.)

When you find a victim, explain that you are going to ask three questions he must answer with his fingers. Then show him how to do it.

First he must make a circle with the thumb and the pinky of his right hand, pressing the nail of the pinky into the underside of the thumb, like this:

Then he must press the three remaining fingers together and place them flat on a table, with the "circle" hanging over the edge, like this:

To answer your first question, he must use the finger closest to the thumb; to answer the second, he must use the second finger, and so on.

To answer "yes," he must wiggle the finger involved. To answer "no," he must raise it an inch or more from the table. But with each answer he must be sure that the other fingers and the "circle" remain in place.

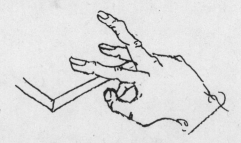

The catch involves the fingers. If he keeps them in the right position, he will find it easy to raise or wiggle the two closest to the thumb, and answer either "yes" or "no" to the first two questions you ask.

But he will find it impossible to raise the third finger. This means that the only answer he can give to the third question is "yes."

And this means that you can make him look slightly silly by choosing the "right" question for him to answer.

Here are three questions to start with:

    1. Do you eat like a pig?
    2. Do you still wash only once a year?
    3. Do you love _____?

Try this trick on a sunny day:
Did you get wet this morning?
No.
You should have washed.

Did you have your TV set on
    yesterday?
Yes.
How did it fit?

Put your finger to your head
    and give the abbreviation for
    "mountain."
M T.
That's right.

Is your refrigerator running?
Yes.
Better go catch it!

I bet I can jump higher
      than a house.
I bet you can't.
Yes, I can. Did you ever see
      a house jump?

Did you ever see a house fly?
Sure. We've got lots of them.
No, not that kind. This kind.
(Draw a picture like this:)

Do you know Tony Chestnut?
No, I don't.
(Moving quickly, step on your friend's
    toes, rap his knees, tap his
    chest, thump his head.)
NOW you do!

Tell your friend you want to tell his fortune. If he agrees, ask him to hold out one of his palms. Stare at it for a second, then follow the creases with one of your fingers. Say, "Here's a crack and here's a crack and there's a crack!" And smack his hand.

Will you help me?
OK.
First raise your head.
Now lower it.
Now turn it to the right.
Now turn it to the left.
Fine.
Now open your mouth.
Now close your mouth.
Now clap your hands.
Now crack your knuckles.
Now close your eyes.
SLAVE!

You'd better keep your eyes open tomorrow.
Why?
You might bump into something if you didn't.

What's the difference between Uncle Sam,
    a rooster, and a bottle of glue? I'll
    give you a hint because this is hard.
    Uncle Sam says, "Yankee doodle do."
    And a rooster says, "Cock-a-doodle-
    do."
And what about the bottle of glue?
That's where you get stuck!

2.

WHAT IS BLACK
AND WHITE
AND RED
ALL OVER?

Most riddles are a test of how good you are at figuring things out. But some of the hardest involve tricks, not reasoning. The answers either make no sense or are so easy no one would expect them to be answers. As a result, they are called catch riddles.

"What is black and white and red all over?" is a good example. The usual answer to this old riddle is, of course, "A newspaper." But there also are others, as you will see.

What is red and goes ding dong?
A red dingdong.
What is white and goes ding dong?
A white dingdong.
What is green and goes ding dong?
A green dingdong.
What is yellow and goes ding dong?
A yellow dingdong.
Oh, no! Wrong! They don't make them
    in that color.

What is white and has a peak and has
    ears?
I don't know.
A snow-covered mountain.
But where are the ears?
You never heard of mountaineers?

What is black and white and red all over?

A chocolate sundae with ketchup on it.

OR

A sunburned zebra.

OR

A blushing zebra.

OR

A skunk with diaper rash.

What is round and purple and hums?
An electric grape.

What has six legs and barks at
    the moon?
I don't know.
A dog.
A dog?
I put two extra legs on it
    to make it harder.

What does a duck do when it flies
    upside down?
It quacks up.

What is gray and has four legs and
a trunk?
A mouse on vacation.

What's this?
(Move your right forefinger around and around
    your right ear. With each turn, stick more and
    more of your other forefinger into your mouth.)
I don't know.
A pencil sharpener sharpening a pencil.

What's this?
(Snapping your fingers, move both hands wildly
    around your head.)
Beats me.
Two butterflies with hiccups.

YOU: A man who lived alone
lost the keys
to his house
and couldn't get in.
He tried the front door,
but it was locked.
Then he tried
the other doors,
but they were locked.
Then he tried the windows,
but they were locked.
Since he was a poor man,
he did not want
to break a window,
and he could not afford
to have a locksmith come.
But finally he managed
to get in anyway.
How did he do it?
YOUR FRIEND: I don't know.
YOU: After he tried
all the doors
and all the windows,
he began to run
around the house.
He ran around

and around
and around
and around
and around
and around
until at last
he was all in.*

* Or, totally tired.

If you were shut up in an iron house
with no windows, no doors, and no other
openings, and you had nothing with you
but a baseball bat, how would you
get out?
I don't know.
Don't you know how to play baseball?
Anybody could get out if he knew how
to play baseball.
You've got me.
It's simple. Three strikes and
you're out.

3.

HAVE YOU THE AUDACITY
TO DOUBT MY VERACITY
AND INSINUATE
THAT I PREVARICATE?

*Nonsense of this sort is called tall talk.
You use big words, long sentences, and large
amounts of hot air to say something simple.
In the example above, it is, "How dare you
call me a liar?"*

*The trick is the unexpected, often funny,
often weird way in which the words themselves are used.*

*But this is also the case with tangletalk,
in which the storyteller may say just the opposite of what he means—"There is no admission, just pay at the door," for instance—
and with other kinds of wordplay as well.*

A	Apple pie
B	Baked it
C	Cut it
D	Divided it
E	Examined it
F	Fought for it
G	Got it
H	Hit at it
I	Eyed it
J	Jumped at it
K	Kicked at it
L	Longed for it
M	Mourned for it
N	Nodded at it
O	Opened it
P	Pursued it
Q	Quartered it
R	Run for it
S	Stood for it
T	Turned it
U	Earned it
V	Viewed it
W	Wanted it
XYZ	Got in and run off— and eat it!

My gastronomical satiety admonishes me that I have arrived at a state of deglutition inconsistent with dietetic integrity.

(Translation: I've had too much to eat.)

A petunia is a flower like a begonia.
A begonia is a meat like a sausage.
A-sausage and battery is a crime.°
Monkeys crime trees.
Trees a crowd.
The rooster crowd and made a lot of noise.
The noise is between the eyes.
Eyes are the opposite of nays.
A horse nays.
A horse also has a colt.
You may go to bed at night with the window open and
    wake up with a colt if you're not careful.

° If you're not a lawyer, this means "assault and battery" which means
deliberately injuring someone.

Two pilots went up in an airplane. The air-
plane had a good motor.
That's good.
No, that's bad. The motor didn't work.
Oh, that's bad.
No, that was good. They had a parachute.
Oh, that's good.

No, that was bad. It didn't open.
That's bad.
No, that was good. There was a
    haystack under them.
That's good.
No, that was bad. There was a
    pitchfork in the haystack.
That's bad.
No, that was good. They missed
    the pitchfork.
That's good.
No, that was bad.
    They missed the haystack.

Ladies and jellybeans,
Reptiles and crocodiles,
I stand before you
  and sit behind you
  to tell you something
  I know nothing about.
There will be a meeting tomorrow night
  right after breakfast
  to decide which color
  to whitewash the church.
There is no admission,
  just pay at the door.
There will be plenty of seats,
  so sit on the floor.

Why are fire engines red?
Roses are red, too.
Two and two are four.
Four and eight are twelve.
There are twelve inches to a ruler.
Queen Mary was a ruler.
Queen Mary was a ship.
Ships sail on the sea.
Fish swim in the sea.
Fish have fins.
The Finns fought the Russians.°
Russians are Reds.
Fire engines are always rushin'.
Which is why fire engines are red.

° Finland and Russia actually have fought off and on for over three hundred years. But this refers to a war in 1939 and 1940.

I'm up here in the nut house.
My mind is in a rut.
My teacher thinks I'm crazy,
But she's just off her nut.
I'm just the same as you are
And I can prove it, too.
Oh, I was born one night one morn
When the whistles went boom boom.
Oh, I can bake a steak or fry a cake
When the mudpies are in bloom.
Oh, six and six makes nine
As ice grows on the vine. . . .
Oh, I'm guilty, Judge, I stole the fudge
And wasn't it just fine. . . .

Oh, the train pulled in the station.
   The bell was ringing wet.
The track ran by the depot,
   And I think it's running yet.

'Twas midnight on the ocean.
   Not a streetcar was in sight.
The sun and moon were shining,
   And it rained all day that night.

'Twas a summer day in winter,
   And the snow was raining fast
As a barefoot boy with shoes on
   Stood sitting on the grass.

Oh, I jumped into the river
   Just because it had a bed.
I took a sheet of water
   For to cover up my head.

Oh, the rain makes all things
     beautiful,
   The flowers and grasses, too.
If the rain makes all things
     beautiful,
   Why don't it rain on you?

Here are two shorter versions of the tangletalk on page 64. They are good examples of how folklore slowly changes as it moves about the land.

'Twas midnight on the ocean.
   Not a streetcar was in sight.
And everything that you could see
   Was hidden out of sight.
'Twas a summer day in winter,
   And the snowflakes fell like glass.
A barefoot boy with shoes on
   Stood sitting in the grass.

'Twas a moonlit day in August.
   The snow was falling fast.
A barefoot boy with shoes on
   Stood sitting in the grass.
The moon shone over the ocean.
   Not a streetcar was in sight.
Someone raised a cloud of dust,
   And it rained all night.

One bright day
in the middle of the night
two dead men
got up to fight.
Back to back
they faced each other,
drew their swords,
and shot each other.
A deaf policeman
heard the noise.
He came and shot
those two dead boys.
If you don't believe
this lie is true,
ask the blind man—
he saw it, too.

4.

THEN THE CAPTAIN
OF THE OTHER YACHT
GOT MAD AND SWORE
AN AWFUL LOT. . . .

There are certain tales which tell a lot but say little, like the one on the next page about the captain of the other yacht and the one on page 74 about the bear that went over the mountain.

At first they sound as if they might be good stories, but sooner or later, usually sooner, they begin repeating the same words or ideas, going around and around, getting nowhere fast.

This is why they are called endless tales or circular tales, or, if they become songs, rounds.° In fact, no one has ever heard how any of these stories end. Nor will you. Nor will your friends. Which is the trick.

° As you go around and around, try to recite these faster and faster.

Then the captain of the *other* yacht

got mad and swore an awful lot.
And the *other* yacht
    gained on the other yacht.
Then the other yacht
    gained on the *other* yacht.
Then the captain of the *other* yacht
    got mad and swore an awful lot.
And the *other* yacht
    gained on the other yacht. . . .

That's *Life!*
What's life?
A magazine.
Where do you get it?
Down at the store.
How much does it cost?
Fifty cents.
Haven't got it.
That's *Life!*
What's life?
A magazine. . . .

Said the boy octopus to the girl octopus: "Let's walk hand in hand in hand in hand in hand in hand. . . ."

It was a dark and stormy night and the captain asked one of the men to tell a story to while away the hours and keep their minds off the frightening noises all about. He began his story:

"It was a dark and stormy night and the captain asked one of the men to tell a story to while away the hours. . . ."

You remind me of a man.
What man?
The man with the power.
What power?
The power to hoodoo.
Who do?
Do what?
Remind me of a man. . . .

Why is the Fourth of July?
Because
J is the first of July and
U is the second of July and
L is the third of July and
Y is the fourth of July.
Because
J is the first of July. . . .

A bear went over the mountain,
A bear went over the mountain,
A bear went over the mountain,
To see what he could see.

He saw another mountain,
He saw another mountain,
He saw another mountain,
And what do you think he did?

He climbed the other mountain,
He climbed the other mountain,
He climbed the other mountain,
And what do you think he saw?

He saw another mountain. . . .

There is another account of the bear's travels. But instead of going around and around, eventually it ends.
The first three stanzas are the same as the ones above. Then things begin to change.

He saw a river in the valley. . . .
    (Repeat three times, then ask:
    "And what do you think he saw?")

He saw a raft in the river. . . .

He saw a shack on the raft. . . .

He saw a man in the shack. . . .

He saw pants on the man. . . .

He saw pockets in the pants. . . .

He saw a nickel in a pocket. . . .

He saw a buffalo on the nickel. . . .°

He saw fur on the buffalo. . . .

He saw a bug in the fur. . . .

He saw glasses on the bug. . . .

He saw cracks in the glass. . . .

He saw water in the cracks. . . .

He saw dirt in the water. . . .

He saw MUD!

° Nickels used to have buffaloes on them.

We met at dawn at the gates of Paris.

And I, being the better man, quickly overcame my adversary.

Whereupon I then retired to a nearby café for proper rest and relaxation.

Whereupon I met a man.

    He said, "What have you been doing?"

    "What have I been doing?"

    "Yes, what have you been doing?"

    "I've been dueling."

    "You've been dueling?"

"Yes, I've been dueling."

"With whom have you been dueling?"

"With whom have I been dueling?"

"Yes, with whom have you been dueling?"

"I've been dueling with Lieutenant Green
      of the Queen's Marines."

"Not Lieutenant Green
      of the Queen's Marines?"

"Yes, Lieutenant Green
      of the Queen's Marines."

"Why, he is my brother!"

"He is your brother?"

"Yes, he is my brother. And we must fight!"

"Must we fight?"

"Yes, we must fight!"

So we met at dawn at the gates of Paris.

And I, being the better man. . . .

Found a peanut, found a peanut.
Found a peanut just now.
Just now I found a peanut,
    found a peanut just now.

Cracked it open, cracked it open.
Cracked it open just now.
Just now I cracked it open,
    cracked it open just now.

It was rotten, it was rotten.
It was rotten just now.
Just now it was rotten,
    it was rotten just now.

Ate it anyway, ate it anyway.
Ate it anyway just now.
Just now I ate it anyway,
    ate it anyway just now.

Got sick, got sick.
Got sick just now.
Just now I got sick,
    got sick just now.

Called a doctor, called a doctor.
Called a doctor just now.
Just now I called a doctor,
    called a doctor just now.

Had an operation, had an operation.
Had an operation just now.
Just now I had an operation,
    had an operation just now.

Feeling better, feeling better.
Feeling better just now.
Just now I'm feeling better,
    feeling better just now.

Found a peanut, found a peanut.
Found a peanut just now. . . .

Once there was a king who was very wise and good. To protect his people against hunger, he decided to store up all the extra grain when the crop was large to make sure there would be food when the crop was small.

So he built great silos all over his kingdom. And soon these were as full of grain as they could be. And the king was very pleased.

But one day a little locust was walking around the bottom of one of the silos and he saw a tiny hole in the wall. And he crawled through the hole, and took a grain of wheat, and crawled out.

Soon he had told all the other locusts about the hole and they all came to the silo.

Then he crawled in and took another grain of wheat.

Then another little locust crawled in and took another grain of wheat.

Then another little locust crawled in and took another grain of wheat.

Then another little locust crawled in and took another grain of wheat.

Then another little locust crawled in and took another grain of wheat.

Then another little locust crawled in. . . .

Pete and Repeat went for a boat ride.
Pete fell in. Who was left?
Repeat.
Pete and Repeat went for a boat ride. . . .

5.

DO YOU HAVE
SOMETHING
TO STOP
THIS COFFIN?

The trick to the endless tales in the last chapter was that they had no ending. The trick to the hoax tales in this chapter is the ending.

There was this rich old miser who died. And he had it in his will to have a lot of money spent on his funeral because he really wanted something grand.

So to be fancy his relatives bought him a big, heavy coffin and got a big, white cart to carry it and a big, white horse to pull the cart.

Well, the cemetery was on a high hill outside of town at the end of a steep gravel road. And when his relatives got partway up, they decided to stop and rest.

But when the horse stopped, something frightened it, and it reared up on its hind legs and jerked the cart so hard the coffin slipped off onto the road.

And when this happened the coffin began sliding back down the hill into town, going faster and faster and faster.

Finally, it tore around a bend in the road, smashed through the window of the drugstore, plowed into the medicine counter, and stopped.

Then the lid popped open, and the miser sat up. "Do you have something to stop this coffin?" he asked.

A customer in a flower shop kept buying roses, eating the blossoms, and throwing away the stems.

"What's wrong with him?" the salesman asked the man's friend.

"He's crazy all right," the friend said. "Everybody knows the stems are the best part."

A lion went for a walk and came upon a small, still pool in which he saw his reflection.

He liked so much what he saw that he decided to find out why the other animals were not as big and strong and beautiful as he was.

The first animal he met was a zebra. "Why is it that you are not as big and strong and beautiful as I am?" he asked. The zebra said he did not know.

The lion then met a hippopotamus and asked him the same question and got the same answer.

Then he met an antelope and asked him, but the antelope did not know either.

Then the lion saw a tiny mouse. "Why is it," he asked, "that you are not as big and strong and beautiful as I am?"

"I've been sick," said the mouse.

Albert Varney was walking down Third Street out toward the country. As he was walking along and thinking, he suddenly realized that it was going to rain.

He looked around for a place to take shelter. But all he could see was an old, dilapidated house that obviously was empty.

Inside, everything was a shambles. But with a flash of lightning and a crash of thunder, the storm was upon him, and he knew it was too late to leave.

Albert then heard a strange rapping sound. It seemed to come from a nearby closet. But nothing was there.

As the rapping grew louder and louder, it gave Albert a very empty feeling, and his efforts to find what was making the sound became more and more frantic.

After searching and searching, he finally decided that the sound was coming from a small trunk. Although he had no trouble unfastening the trunk, getting up enough nerve to open it was a different matter.

However, he soon overcame his fear, jerked open the lid, and looked inside. At last he knew what was making the dreadful rapping sound.

It was wrapping paper.

There were two skunks—
   Out and In.
When In was out,
   Out was in.
One day Out was in
   and In was out.
Their mother,
   who was in with Out,
   wanted In in.
"Bring In in,"
   she said to Out.
So Out went out
   and brought In in.
"How did you find him
   so fast?" she asked.
"Instinct," he said.

One night a man paid his friend a visit and, much to his surprise, found him playing chess with his dog.

"This dog must be very intelligent to be able to play chess," he said.

"Oh, he's not so smart," his friend replied. "I just beat him three games out of four."

As we were coming home from the show one night, we saw George sitting in front of the soda shop all out of breath and sweating like a panther.

He had a tired look on his face and appeared to have been running for some time. When we asked him what was wrong, he told us this story:

"I was walking past the insane asylum just about a half hour ago, and as I went by the gate a horrible-looking maniac with a long knife jumped out in front of me.

"Of course, I was scared and I wasted no time in starting to run. I don't know how far I ran or how fast, but I was able to keep away from him for a while.

"Then my strength began giving out and he started gaining on me. And every once in a while he would wave his knife and let out this horrible scream.

"He was no more than ten feet behind me when I stumbled over a large rock and fell. And a million thoughts of what might happen flashed through my head.

"Then he reached down and grabbed me by my neck. And the next thing I knew I was on my feet looking into his eyes.

"He stared at me for a minute, then tapped me on the shoulder, and said:

" 'TAG, YOU RASCAL!' "

This was when my grandfather and Admiral Perry were at the North Pole. The two of them and one of their friends got separated from their group and got caught in a blizzard.

During the night their friend froze to death. When the other two woke up the next morning, they decided to bury him in the ice.

So they measured him and found he was six feet long. And they started to cut a hole that size.

When they finally got finished, they put their friend in, and they were all sad and everything.

Only they found that the hole was too long. So they pulled it out of the ice and sawed off the extra inches and put it back in.

But then they stuck it in upside down. So they had to take it out and make another one.

There was this middle-aged man who lived all by himself in a large city. His name was Jake Smith. Jake was very lonesome because his wife was dead and he had no children.

One night Jake was so lonely he went out and got drunk. About midnight he came wobbling home. There was not a star in the sky and the wind whistled through the trees.

His house was one of three which were exactly alike. However, he managed to choose the right one and began to stagger toward it.

But suddenly he became aware of a strange noise. And when he looked around, he saw a white coffin bouncing along behind him.

He was so frightened that he immediately became sober and ran up the porch steps as fast as he could. Meanwhile, the coffin had turned in at the gate and was coming slowly toward him.

Jake fumbled among his keys until he found the right one. Then he quickly unlocked the door, rushed inside, and locked it again.

But when he looked out the window the coffin was already on the porch. It paused in front of the door, and then, with a horrible crash, smashed into the house.

As Jake scampered up the stairs to the second floor, the coffin bumped across the living room after him.

But when it started up the stairs, something seemed to stop it. Several times it tried, but each time it fell back. Then suddenly it managed to climb the first step, then the second, then the third.

Jake held his breath. Somehow he knew that if it managed to get all the way up, he would be a goner. He picked up a chair and threw it at the coffin, hoping to knock it down. But instead something knocked the chair away, and it broke into a hundred pieces.

Then Jake had a great idea. He hurried into his bedroom, got a small, square box from his dresser, and rushed back to the top of the stairs.

Quickly he opened the box, took out a cough drop, and threw it at the coffin.

And the coffin stopped.

Two horses were standing in the middle of a field
discussing current events.

A dog wandered over and asked, "What's new, fellows?"

One of the horses turned to the other with a surprised
look on his face.

"Imagine that," he said, "a talking dog."

One day my father was riding down this old country road on his horse. It was just after a bad rainstorm.

Suddenly he saw this man's head sticking out of the mud right next to the road. He couldn't believe it, but it was true.

"Hello!" said the man, smiling.

"Oh, my heavens!" said Daddy. "What happened to you? Wait! Hold on! I'll get some rope and maybe I can pull you out of there."

"Oh, that's all right," said the man. "I'm standing on a ladder."

Three polar bears awakened from their long winter's nap on an iceberg.

Papa Bear stood up and stretched and announced: "I have a tale to tell."

Mama Bear stood up and stretched and announced: "I have a tale to tell."

But Baby Bear just sat on the ice shivering.

"My tale is told," he said.

Notes and Sources
Bibliography
An Acknowledgment

ABBREVIATIONS IN NOTES AND SOURCES

CFQ   *California Folklore Quarterly*

HF   *Hoosier Folklore*

HFB   *Hoosier Folklore Bulletin*

JA   Louis C. Jones Archives, New York State Historical Association, Cooperstown. Folklore collected in the 1940s by students at Albany State Teachers College, N.Y., now Albany State College, under the direction of Professor Louis C. Jones.

JAF   *Journal of American Folklore*

KFQ   *Keystone Folklore Quarterly*

LC   Library of Congress, Folk Song Section, Washington, D.C. Includes the WPA Folklore Archives assembled state by state in the 1930s during the great economic depression. Collectors were unemployed folklorists and writers hired by the federal government.

MA   Maryland Folklore Archives, University of Maryland, College Park. Includes student collections dating to the 1960s.

MF   *Midwest Folklore*

NYFQ   *New York Folklore Quarterly*

SFQ   *Southern Folklore Quarterly*

TA   Harold W. Thompson Archive, New York State Historical Association, Cooperstown. Folklore collected in the 1940s and 1950s by Cornell University students under the direction of Professor Harold W. Thompson.

TFSB   *Tennessee Folklore Society Bulletin*

UPA   University of Pennsylvania Folklore Archives, Philadelphia. Includes student collections dating to the 1960s.

WF   *Western Folklore*

WSA   Wayne State University Folklore Archive, Detroit. Includes student collections dating to the 1960s.

NOTES AND SOURCES

The verbal trickery in this book has many sources: my childhood, my children, their friends; other children I interviewed in New Jersey, Pennsylvania, and Maine; the folklore archives and publications listed on page 104, and, of course, folklorists themselves.

The source of each trick is given. So are the names of the collector and informant, when available, and any background. The bibliography contains complete information on the publications cited.

1.
IF FROZEN WATER
IS ICED WATER,
WHAT IS
FROZEN INK?

p. 15 *If frozen water.* Iona and Peter Opie, *The Lore and Language of Schoolchildren,* p. 58. A catch found both in England and northeastern United States.

p. 16 *Take any number.* Various archives.

Please add these. Learned as a counselor, Camp Alton,

Wolfeboro, N.H., late 1940s. Opie, *The Lore and Language of Schoolchildren*, p. 65, contains an English version.

If three pigeons. Carl Sandburg, *Abraham Lincoln: The Prairie Years*, v. 2, p. 81.

p. 17 *If you were walking in a field*. MA, 1971.

p. 18 *I know a fellow*. Learned as a teen-ager, Brooklyn, N.Y., early 1940s. A variant is reported by Carl A. Withers, "Current Events in New York City Children's Folklore," a summary of research among Brooklyn College freshmen (*NYFQ* 3, p. p. 213).

I bet I can jump. TA, 1940s.

Is your house. JA, Marianne Adams, 1945.

p. 19 *Ask me if I'm a boat*, TA, 1940s.

p. 20 *My mother sent me*. JA, Edna Kirkpatrick, 1945.

p. 22 *I one it*. Various archives, publications. Traditional catch.

Do you know something? JA, Edna Kirkpatrick, 1945.

p. 23 *Will you remember me*. Reported by Nancy Schwartz, 14, Elizabeth Schwartz, 12, Princeton, N.J., 1972.

p. 24 *If I lived up here*. Collected at Belmont School, Philadelphia, 1971. Also Roger D. Abrahams, "The Catch in Negro Philadelphia," *KFQ* 8, p. 107.

p. 25 *Would you hit someone*. Various archives. Also Carl A. Withers, "Current Events in New York City Children's Folklore," *NYFQ* 3, p. 213. A variant reported by Peter Bernard, 14, Princeton, N.J., 1971:

A says: If you hit me, I won't hit you back.
B hits A.
A hits B "in front," not "in back."
Hey, your shirttail's. UPA, John B. Fisher, Paradise, Pa., 1964.
Watch out! Reported by Nancy Fish, 12, Concord, Mass., 1972.

p. 26 *Would you like to join.* JA, Robert Sullivan, 1945. In other versions (JA, 1945) the "Siamese" words are: "Wha ta goo Siam!"; "Wha ta dough pie yam!"

I can make you into. Collected at John Witherspoon School, Princeton, N.J., 1972. Also David J. Winslow, "An Annotated Collection of Children's Folklore," *KFQ* 11, p. 171.

p. 27 *Don't touch the baby.* JA, 1945.

p. 28 *The Golden Arm.* MA, 1970. This version of an old "scare story" was tape-recorded by an anonymous collector in Maryland. It has been adapted for clarity. The tale has uncounted variants and has been known for generations in Europe and in North America. John Burrison dates its arrival in the United States from Europe to roughly 1800, in *The Golden Arm: The Folk Tale and Its Literary Use by Mark Twain and Joel C. Harris,* p. 15. The comment from Mark Twain is from Thomas H. English, *Mark Twain to Uncle Remus,* as quoted in Burrison. In the Aarne-Thompson classification of folk tales, "The Golden Arm" is categorized as Tale Type 366, "The Man from the Gallows," in which a corpse returns to punish the theft of one of its possessions, including parts of its body.

p. 31 *Do you collect stamps?* JA, Anna Becker, 1945.

p. 32 *Three little monkeys sat on a fence.* JA, Mary-Jean Carver, 1945. One of several catches (including "If three pigeons," p. 16, and "Pete and Repeat," p. 83) which rely on a formula in the traditional "Adam and Eve" trap: Adam and Eve and Pinchme (or Nipmehard, Nipmewell, Sockmyjaw, Punchmyknees, or Treadonmytoes) went down to the river to swim (or went for a boat ride or sat on a fence). Adam and Eve drowned (or fell in the water or fell off the fence). And who was left?

When the response is "Pinchme" or "Nipmewell" or one of the others, tricksters in one English town reply, "It's a pleasure!" Opie, *The Lore and Language of Schoolchildren*, p. 59, collected in Presteigne, England.

p. 33 *Just like me.* Various archives, publications. Traditional catch.

p. 34 *What does a ship do.* JA, 1945. Also Opie, *The Lore and Language of Schoolchildren*, p. 57, collected in Lydney, England.

I know what you're going to say. William C. Hazlitt, *Studies in Jocular Literature*, p. 26.

I bet I can make you say "black." Reported by Nancy Schwartz, 14, Elizabeth Schwartz, 12, Princeton, N.J., 1972.

p. 35 *I bet you can't stick.* UPA, Janet M. Kagarise, 1964.

p. 36 *The three questions.* From a brief synopsis in Alan Dundes's "Some Minor Genres of American Folklore," *SFQ* 31, p. 24.

p. 38 *Did you get wet this morning?* Opie, *The Lore and Language of Schoolchildren,* p. 67, collected in Ipswich, England; Maine, and New Jersey.

Did you have your TV set on. MA, 1967.

Put your finger to your head. UPA, Janet M. Kagarise, 1964.

p. 39 *Is your refrigerator running?* MA, 1968. In this version the question is asked face to face. In a variant (WSA, 1969) the trickster telephones his question, then offers to head the refrigerator off at the corner.

p. 40 *I bet I can jump.* TA, 1940s.

Did you ever see a house fly? MA, Patrick Lister, 1967.

p. 41 *Do you know Tony Chestnut?* An old chestnut reported by children in Philadelphia and in Princeton, N.J., 1972.

p. 42 *Here's a crack.* UPA, Janet M. Kagarise, 1964.

Will you help me? JA, Mary Honcharnik, and Boris Glus, 1945. Adapted from a synopsis.

p. 43 *You'd better keep your eyes open.* JA, Roberta Jobson, 1945.

What's the difference between. LC, unnamed location in Michigan, 1930s.

2.
WHAT IS BLACK
AND WHITE
AND RED
ALL OVER?

p. 46 *What is red and goes ding dong?* MA, S. K. Gregory, 1970. In another version the question is, "What is red and goes boo boo?" and the answer is, "A red booboo."

What is white and has a peak and has ears? TA, 1945.

p. 47 *What is black and white.* Chocolate sundae: MA, Mary Lee Burbage, 1968; zebras: students at Rutgers University, 1971; skunk: Ellie Heymann, 12, Princeton, N.J., 1972.

p. 48 *What is round.* Reported in Mac E. Barrick, "The Shaggy Elephant Riddle," *SFQ* 28, p. 266.

What has six legs. Brian Sutton-Smith, "The Folk Games of the Children," in T. Coffin, ed., *Our Living Traditions: An Introduction to American Folklore,* p. 189.

What does a duck do. MA, Barbara Crampton, 1967.

p. 49 *What is gray and has four legs.* Various archives. One of a cycle of "What's it?" riddles that were popular in the United States and Canada in the early 1960s.

p. 50 *What's this?* These catch riddles are the only tricks in this book that do not rely on words. Instead they rely on sign language. Folklorists call them non-oral riddles. The "pencil sharpener" and the "butterflies" have been circulating at least since

1950 when I learned them as a student at North-western University in Illinois. Jan Harold Brun-vand describes these and others he collected in the Middle West during the 1950s: "More Non-Oral Riddles," *WF* 19, p. 132.

p. 51 *A man who lived alone.* TA, 1945. Because of the dreadful pun with which it ends, this tale could be classified as a hoax tale or shaggy dog story of the type in Chapter 5. See the note to p. 85. Yet it seems more at home as a riddle.

p. 53 *If you were shut up in an iron house.* LC, New York City, 1938. In another version there is a locked door, and the hero plays a piano until he finds the right key to unlock it.

3.
HAVE YOU THE AUDACITY
TO DOUBT MY VERACITY
AND INSINUATE
THAT I PREVARICATE?

p. 55 *Have you the audacity.* J. M. Garrett, Houston, Texas, 1954.

p. 56 *A—Apple pie.* Paul G. Brewster *et al.,* "Children's Games and Rhymes," *Frank C. Brown Collection of North Carolina Folklore,* v. 1, p. 174. Contrib-uted by Minnie Stamps Gosney, Wake County, N.C. Adapted slightly.

This item and several others in this chapter are chain tales in which the storyteller adds new information according to a fixed pattern, e.g., with each line or stanza.

p. 57 *My gastronomical satiety.* UPA, Mary Ellen Brown Lewis, Indiana, Pa., 1964.

p. 58 *A petunia is a flower.* TA, 1945. Adapted for clarity.

p. 59 *Two pilots went up.* Lee Martin, "Dialogue," *HF* 7, p. 21. The "good-bad" pattern in this chain tale is categorized in the Aarne-Thompson classification of folk tales as Type 2014A, "The House Burned Down."

p. 61 *Ladies and jellybeans.* JA, Harriet Abrams, 1945.

p. 62 *Why are fire engines red?* Various archives.

p. 63 *I'm up here in the nut house.* MA, Andrea Weatherby, 1967. Fragment of a traditional camp song incorporating tangletalk.

p. 64 *Oh, the train pulled in.* Various archives.

p. 66 *'Twas midnight on the ocean.* TA, 1940s.
'Twas a moonlit day in August. JA, Marianne Adams, 1945.

p. 67 *One bright day.* UPA, George G. Miller, Ardmore, Pa., 1961.

4.
THEN THE CAPTAIN
OF THE OTHER YACHT
GOT MAD AND SWORE
AN AWFUL LOT. . . .

p. 69 Endless tale, circular tale. Whether a tale is "endless" or "circular" depends on how far it progresses before it begins again. The shorter its cycle, the more likely is it to be regarded as endless. Of course, how one defines the difference also may depend on how much repetition he can bear.

p. 70 *Then the captain.* Richard K. Beardsley, "Circular Jingles," *WF* 6, p. 86. Adapted slightly for clarity.

p. 71 *That's Life!* Various archives. A tale that began to circulate soon after *Life* magazine first appeared in 1936. The earliest accounts gave the cost as a nickel or a dime. But as the price rose, this was reflected in later versions. *Life* ceased publication in 1972. Whether this will affect use of the tale remains to be seen.

Said the boy octopus. Various archives. This endless tale is based on a Wellerism, a folklore genre in which a common saying or proverb—in this case, "hand in hand"—is combined with an unexpected idea. The result ranges from peculiar to hilarious, depending on how one sees things. " 'So long,' said the chimp as he slid down the giraffe's neck" is another example. " 'Delighted,' said the firefly as he backed into the fan" is still another.

Wellerisms are named for Sam Weller, a character in Charles Dickens's *The Pickwick Papers* (1837) who used this form endlessly. But scholars also have found it in ancient Greek and Roman literature. Archer Taylor, "Wellerisms," *Standard Dictionary of Folklore, Mythology, and Legend,* v. 2, p. 1169.

p. 72 *It was a dark and stormy night.* Various archives. One of the traditional circular tales and songs which thrive at summer camps for young people. In some versions the leader is an army officer or a sea captain. In others he is an Indian chief or the head of a band of thieves.

p. 73 *You remind me of a man.* From Belmont School, Philadelphia, 1971. This migrant from Negro tradition in the South also has been reported in New York by Alta Jablow and Carl A. Withers, "Social Sense and Verbal Nonsense in Urban Children's Folklore," *NYFQ* 21, p. 243. In 1947 it was used in a movie, *The Bachelor and the Bobby-Soxer.*

Why is the Fourth of July? J. R. Caldwell, "Folk-Rhymes," *CFQ* 3, p. 319.

p. 74 *A bear went over the mountain.* The two versions presented are traditional at summer camps. The first is a circular tale or round. The second is a chain tale. See the note to p. 56. I learned both as a camper in 1940 at the Ten Mile River Boy Scout Camps in New York State. Some years later, as a camp counselor, I taught them to children at Camp Alton, Wolfeboro, N.H.

Professor Alta Jablow of Brooklyn College collected a variant of the chain tale in 1962 from a fourteen-year-old Brooklyn girl who also had learned it at camp. It is reported in "Social Sense and Verbal Nonsense in Urban Children's Folklore," *NYFQ* 21, p. 243, and reproduced in Carl A. Withers, *I Saw a Rocket Walk a Mile*, p. 42.

p. 77 *We met at dawn.* Dan G. Hoffman, "Half a Dozen
Repeating Games," *NYFQ* 4, p. 207.

p. 79 *Found a peanut.* Various archives.

p. 81 *Once there was a king.* UPA, Sallie Bannister, 1964.
Miss Bannister learned this version of a traditional endless tale as a child in the 1940s from her
grandmother in Lima, Ohio. Her grandmother
had learned it about 1910 from her husband. It is
a good example of how folklore is transmitted
within a family. Adapted slightly for clarity.

p. 83 *Pete and Repeat went out.* Various archives.

5.
DO YOU HAVE
SOMETHING
TO STOP
THIS COFFIN?

p. 85 Hoax tale. Also a shaggy dog story or a sell. Often a
long, tedious tale, but in any case one whose con-
clusion is absurd or pointless. Jan Harold Brunvand, "A Classification of Shaggy Dog Stories,"
JAF 76, p. 42.

p. 86 *There was this rich old miser.* MA, Barbara Hines and
Robert Mardres, 1971. Adapted from a synopsis.

p. 88 *A customer in a flower shop.* JA, 1945.

p. 89 *A lion went for a walk.* Various archives, publications.
In some versions the lion is an elephant and the
mouse is an ant. In a five-thousand-year-old
Sumerian fable the final dialogue is between an

elephant ("There is nothing like me in all creation") and a wren ("In my own small way I was created just as you were"). Samuel N. Kramer, *History Begins at Sumer* (1959), p. 132, as quoted in J. H. Brunvand, "A Classification of Shaggy Dog Stories," *JAF* 76, p. 42.

p. 90 *Albert Varney was walking.* Ernest W. Baughman and Clayton S. Holaday, "Tall Tales and 'Sells' from Indiana University Students," *HFB* 3, p. 59. Also various archives. Adapted slightly for clarity. In other versions the old house is a hotel and the wrapping paper is a huge roll of wrapping paper. Listed by Brunvand, "A Classification of Shaggy Dog Stories," as Type C665, "The Rapping Paper." See note to p. 85.

p. 91 *There were two skunks.* JA, 1945.

p. 92 *One night a man.* JA, 1945.

p. 93 *As we were coming home.* Baughman and Holaday, see note to p. 88. Also various archives. Adapted slightly for clarity. Variants have been reported in Maine (Richard M. Dorson, *American Folklore*, p. 131) and in Texas and Mexico (Américo Paredes: "Tag, You're It," *JAF* 73, p. 157. Brunvand Type D100, "Encounter with a Horrible Monster."

p. 95 *This was when my grandfather.* MA, 1970. Adapted slightly for clarity.

p. 96 *There was this middle-aged man.* Baughman and Holaday, see note to p. 88. Also various archives.

Adapted slightly for clarity. Brunvand Type C620, "The Walking Coffin." ·

p. 99 *Two horses were standing.* JA, 1945.

p. 100 *One day my father was riding.* MA, 1970.

p. 102 *Three polar bears awakened.* MA, Barbara Hines and Robert L. David, 1971. Based on a Wellerism. See note to p. 69, *Said the boy octopus.*

BIBLIOGRAPHY

BOOKS

Books of particular interest to young people are marked with an asterisk (°).

Books marked with a dagger (†) are sources of detailed information on endless tales, chain tales, hoax stories, and other "formula" material.

† Aarne, Antti, and Thompson, Stith. *The Types of the Folk-Tale*. Folklore Fellows Communications No. 184. Second revision. Helsinki, Finland, 1961. Types 2000–2350.

° Botkin, Benjamin A. *Treasury of American Folklore*. New York: Crown Publishers, 1944.

Brewster, Paul G., *et al.*, ed. *Children's Games and Rhymes*. Frank C. Brown Collection of North Carolina Folklore, v. 1. Durham, N.C.: Duke University Press, 1952.

Burrison, John A. *The Golden Arm: The Folk Tale and Its Literary Use by Mark Twain and Joel C. Harris*. Research Paper 19. Atlanta, Ga.: Georgia State College, 1968.

° Charlip, Remy. *Arm in Arm*. New York: Parents' Magazine Press, 1969. *A brief collection of endless and circular tales.*

Dorson, Richard M. *American Folklore*. Chicago: University of Chicago Press, 1959.

° Emrich, Duncan. *The Nonsense Book*. New York: Four Winds Press, 1970.

Hazlitt, William C. *Studies in Jocular Literature*. London: E. Stock, 1890.

Johnson, Clifton. *What They Say in New England and Other American Folklore*. Boston: Lee and Shepherd, 1896. Reprint, ed. Carl A. Withers. New York: Columbia University Press, 1963. *One of the first comprehensive collections of folklore in the United States.*

° Justus, May T. *The Complete Peddler's Pack: Games, Songs, Rhymes & Riddles from Mountain Folklore*. Knoxville, Tenn.: University of Tennessee Press, 1967.

° Leach, Maria. *Noodles, Nitwits, and Numskulls*. Cleveland and New York: World Publishing Co., 1961.

° ———. *Riddle Me, Riddle Me, Ree*. New York: The Viking Press, 1970.

Opie, Iona and Peter. *The Lore and Language of Schoolchildren*. London and New York: Oxford University Press, 1959. *A classic account of children's folklore in England and Scotland.*

Sandburg, Carl. *Abraham Lincoln: The Prairie Years*. Vol. 2. New York: Harcourt, Brace & Company, 1928.

Standard Dictionary of Folklore, Mythology, and Legend. Ed. Maria Leach. 2 vols. New York: Funk & Wagnalls, 1949.

Thompson, Stith. *The Folktale*. New York: Holt, Rinehart & Winston, 1946.

† ————. *Motif-Index of Folk-Literature*. 6 vols. Bloomington, Ind.: Indiana University Press, 1955–58. *Motifs Z0-Z99.*

° Withers, Carl A. *I Saw a Rocket Walk a Mile*. New York: Holt, Rinehart & Winston, 1965. *An outstanding book of formula tales from throughout the world.*

° ————. *A Rocket in My Pocket: The Rhymes and Chants of Young Americans*. New York: Holt, Rinehart & Winston, 1948.

ARTICLES

Articles marked with a dagger (†) are sources of detailed information on endless tales, chain tales, hoax stories, and other "formula" material.

Abrahams, Roger D. "The Catch in Negro Philadelphia." *KFQ* 8 (1963):107.

Barrick, Mac E. "The Shaggy Elephant Riddle." *SFQ* 28 (1964):266.

Baughman, Ernest W., and Holaday, Clayton S. "Tall Tales and 'Sells' from Indiana University Students." *HFB* 3 (1944):59.

Beardsley, Richard K. "Circular Jingles." *WF* 6 (1947):86.

† Brunvand, Jan Harold. "A Classification of Shaggy Dog Stories." *JAF* 76 (1963):42.

————. "More Non-Oral Riddles." *WF* 19 (1960):132.

Caldwell, J. R. "Folk-Rhymes." *CFQ* 3 (1944):319.

Cansler, Loman D. "Midwestern and British Children's Lore Compared." *WF* 27 (1968):1.

Cray, Ed, and Herzog, Marilyn E. "The Absurd Elephant: A Recent Riddle Fad." *WF* 26 (1963):27.

Cray, Ed. and Leventhal, Nancy C. "Depth Collecting from a Sixth Grade Class." *WF* 22 (1963):159, 231. *In a three-month period thirty-one pupils in a sixth grade class in Hawthorne, California, contributed 363 distinct folklore items and 3,397 variants. The items included superstitions, rhymes, songs, riddles, tongue twisters, tricks, taunts, insults, and jokes, which Mrs. Leventhal used to enrich her teaching in English and social studies.*

Dundes, Alan. "The Elephant Joking Question." *TFSB* 29 (1963):2.

———. "On Game Morphology: A Study of the Structure of Non-Verbal Folktales." *NYFQ* 20 (1964):276.

———. "Some Minor Genres of American Folklore." *SFQ* 31 (1967):24.

Hoffman, Dan G. "Half a Dozen Repeating Games." *NYFQ* 4 (1948):207.

Jablow, Alta, and Withers, Carl A. "Social Sense and Verbal Nonsense in Urban Children's Folklore." *NYFQ* 21 (1965):243.

Koch, William E. "Wellerisms from Kansas." *WF* 18 (1959):180.

Martin, Lee. "Dialogue." *HF* 7 (1948):21.

Paredes, Américo. "Tag, You're It." *JAF* 73 (1960):157.

Porter, Kenneth. "Circular Jingles and Repetitious Rhymes." *WF* 17 (1958):107.

———. "Some Central Kansas Wellerisms." *MF* 8 (1958): 158.

Sutton-Smith, Brian. "The Folk Games of the Children," in *Our Living Traditions: An Introduction to American Folklore*. Ed. Tristram Potter Coffin. New York and London: Basic Books, 1968.

† Taylor, Archer. "A Classification of Formula Tales." *JAF* 46 (1933):77.

———. "Wellerisms." *Standard Dictionary of Folklore, Mythology, and Legend*, vol. 2.

Winslow, David J. "An Annotated Collection of Children's Folklore." *KFQ* 11 (1966):171.

Withers, Carl A. "Current Events in New York City Children's Folklore." *NYFQ* 3 (1947):213.

AN ACKNOWLEDGMENT

The following persons and organizations shared their knowledge with me during the research for this book:

Professor Bruce R. Buckley and Mrs. Marion Brophey, Cooperstown Graduate Programs, New York State Historical Association; Professor John A. Burrison, Georgia State College; Joseph C. Hickerson, librarian, Folk Song Section, Library of Congress.

Professor Esther K. Birdsall, Mrs. Geraldine Johnson, and Nathan Olivera, University of Maryland; Professors Kenneth S. Goldstein and Dan Ben-Amos, University of Pennsylvania; Norma W. Portwood, Wayne State University.

The folklore students whose research and recollections I was privileged to review at many folklore archives.

The children at Belmont School in Philadelphia and at John Witherspoon School in Princeton, New Jersey, who introduced me to their tricks, traps, and tales.

Peter, Nancy, and Elizabeth Schwartz, who helped me decide what to include in this book and what to leave out.

The Princeton University Library, the Princeton Public Library, the libraries at Rutgers University and the University of Maine.

The folklore societies and the publishing firms which provided permission to use copyrighted materials.

To each I am deeply grateful.

A. S.

ABOUT THE AUTHOR

ALVIN SCHWARTZ was born in Brooklyn, New York, and now lives in Princeton, New Jersey, with his wife, children and two cats. The author of many books for young people and adults, he has written six books whose specific aim is, as he says, "to heighten in young people an awareness of folklore and its role in our culture, yet meet scholarly requirements." Those books include *Kickle Snifters and Other Fearsome Critters*, *Whoppers*, *Cross Your Fingers, Spit in Your Hat*, *Witcracks*, *A Twister of Twists, a Tangler of Tongues*, cited by *The New York Times* as one of the best children's books of 1972, and *Tomfoolery*, cited by *The New York Times* as one of the best children's books of 1973. He has researched and written many books for young people which explore American institutions and aspects of Political Science and Sociology. Mr. Schwartz appears frequently as a principal speaker concerning children's literature, discussing humor, childlore and folklore at conferences throughout the country.

ABOUT THE ILLUSTRATOR

GLENN ROUNDS spent his childhood on ranches in South Dakota and Montana. He attended art school in Kansas City, Missouri, and in New York City, and now lives in Southern Pines, North Carolina. He has illustrated many books for young people, and has collaborated with Alvin Schwartz often, including illustrating the highly acclaimed *A Twister of Twists, a Tangler of Tongues*, and most recently, *Tomfoolery*.